STUPID KIDS

BY JOHN C. RUSSELL

D1564001

★

★

DRAMATISTS
PLAY SERVICE
INC.

SPECIAL NOTE

SPECIAL NOTE ON SONGS AND RECORDINGS

STUPID KIDS was produced by WPA Theatre (Kyle Renick, Artistic Director; Lori Sherman, Managing Director), The Shubert Organization, ABC, Inc., Scott Rudin, Roger Berlind, and Robert Fox, at the Century Theatre, in New York City, on August 24, 1998. It was directed by Michael Mayer; the set design was by David Gallo; the costume design was by Michael Krass; the lighting design was by Kevin Adams; the sound design was by Laura Grace Brown; the musical staging was by Ken Roberson; and the production stage manager was Bradley McCormick. The cast was as follows:

JUDY NOONAN .... Shannon Burkett
JIM STARK .... James Carpinello
JOHN "NEECHEE" CRAWFORD .... Keith Nobbs
JANE "KIMBERLY" WILLIS .... Mandy Siegfried

This production of STUPID KIDS received its premiere at WPA Theatre (Kyle Renick, Artistic Director; Lori Sherman, Managing Director) in New York City, on June 1, 1998.

TABLE OF CONTENTS

CHARACTERS

JIM STARK — 17, tough, rebellious, self-impressed, new in town.
JUDY NOONAN — 17, the girl.
JOHN "NEECHEE" CRAWFORD — 17, lonely, angry, queer.
JANE "KIMBERLY" WILLIS — 17, lonely, angry, queer.
VOICES — Four cops. Crunch [one actor, or recorded voices].

PLACE

The burbs.

TIME

First through eighth period, the rest of the day, day in day out.

The "Music Video" scenes are stylized movement pieces performed live, in imitation of music videos and/or teen film montage sequences.

STUPID KIDS

SCENE ONE

MUSIC VIDEO #1*

The actors are in isolated spots on stage. They are all at the same large party on a Saturday night. They are drinking and doing drugs. As the song progresses, Jim gets angry and violent, Judy flirts then fights boys off, Neechee gets paranoid and starts to freak out, Kimberly steals from partygoers and the house. They use such motions as: Step, touch; arms up; kicks to side; air guitars.

Towards the end of the song, cop car lights focus and all four dash madly about, escaping/hiding from the cops. They all end in a line — Jim, Neechee, Kimberly, Judy — all in the police station. Cops are all offstage voices.

*Suggested music: "Stupid Kids" by Dan Selzman, Elizabeth Gox, Michael Cudahy and Peter Rutigliano. Performed by Christmas. See Special Note on Music on copyright page.

SCENE TWO

INTERROGATIONS

JIM.   *(Kimberly and Judy turn U.)* Fuck you, man. Fuck all of you.

COP 1.   That kind of talk is not going to help you, Mr. Stark.

JIM.   Fuck it. *(Jim turns U. Judy turns D.)*

JUDY.   *(Adjusting her skirt.)* This is not fucking provocative. Shit.

COP 2.   Young lady, that was unnecessary.

JUDY.   Judy. This is what — there were tons of girls dressed like this out tonight, at that party. *(Judy turns U. Kimberly turns D.)*

KIMBERLY.   I don't believe in private property.

COP 3.   That is not for you to believe or not believe in. There are laws.

KIMBERLY.   Fuck the laws. *(Neechee strokes his hair. Kimberly's hands are in her back pockets facing U. Judy's hands are on her head facing U. Jim's arms are crossed facing U.)*

COP 4.   John ... John? Do you have any idea why you shot those puppies? John? *(Neechee strokes his hair again.)*

NEECHEE.   No.

COP 4.   John ... Is that what they call you, or do you have a nickname?

NEECHEE.   They call me Neechee. Like the fucked-up philosopher. 'Cept we spell it phonetically so it's more accessible. *(Pause.)*

COP 4.   Neechee, why don't you try to remember what made you kill those puppies.

NEECHEE.   I don't fucking know why, OK? Fuck! I did it! I fuckin' confess! River of blood — disaster. You want the facts? ... Those are the facts. *(Sad.)* But I don't know why, OK? Why the fuck does it matter to *you* why? It's not your fuckin' problem. *(Kimberly facing U. Neechee turns U., hands on wall. Judy facing U. hand on hip, hand on head. Jim turns D.)*

JIM.   You wanna know why? I'll tell ya why. The whole world is fucked, that's why. I can't do drugs or even drink beer in front of the fuckin' tube like my old man without gettin' busted. We fuckin' moved here cuz my parents thought bein' Jimmy in the corner was the only way to keep my nose clean — no tit to lick, no butt to kick. But if you want trouble, trouble seeks you out. Always some fire burning somewhere. *(Jim turns U. Kimberly turns D.)*

KIMBERLY. It's wrong to steal, yes, so they tell me. But it's nice to share. So how's about I share what I steal? Huh? Would you like that? Cuz I would. I would share indiscriminately. I would share inappropriately and rebelliously. I would share creatively. Cuz I'm not taking so I can have things. I'm taking so I can fuck with your brain. *(Kimberly turns U. with hands on hood. Judy turns D.)*

JUDY. I never dreamed something like this could happen to me. I go to a party, get poked at. I get some jerk's "McDonald's grease hands" and rum and Coke tongue on my breasts and in my mouth. I feel dirty, alone. And then you blame me because my dress is short.

COP 2. There's nothing we can do about it, Miss Noonan, if you're not going to name names. *(Judy turns. All cross U.)* Why don't we just call your parents?

ALL. *(All turn D.)* My parents! *(All cross D.)* No, you can't call my parents. You can't! *(Start 4 cts. into music: Kimberly crosses U.C.R., Judy crosses R. Neechee sits L. Jim crosses U.C.L. They all take a step forward. They are in a waiting room. These scenes are between same sex pairs, played simultaneously.)*

JIM AND KIMBERLY. *(Music ends.)* You look cold. *(Kimberly takes off her jacket.)* Do you want my jacket? It's warm.

NEECHEE AND JUDY. No. No, thank you. *(Neechee crosses to Jim and Kimberly crosses to Judy giving her the jacket. Pause.)* I'm scared. *(Kimberly and Jim cross to Judy and Neechee.)*

JIM AND KIMBERLY. No reason to be scared of me. *(Judy puts on the jacket.)*

JIM. My name is Jim Stark *(Handshake.)*

KIMBERLY. *(Neechee leans on the wall L. Jim U. of Neechee.)* My name is Kimberly. It's really Jane, and I know Kimberly sounds like a mall chick name, but Kimberly is the name of Patti Smith's kid sister and that's who I am. Spiritually.

JUDY. I'm Judy. *(Handshake.)* Who's Patti Smith?
KIMBERLY. You don't have any older brothers or sisters, do you?
JUDY. No, I'm an only child.
KIMBERLY. Well, I can teach you all about Patti Smith and the rebellious '70s. If you want to learn.
JUDY. Sure. *(Judy sits. Kimberly squats.)*
NEECHEE. My name's Neechee.
JIM. *(Jim puts the jacket on Neechee.)* Huh. But that's not your real name.
NEECHEE. No, my real name's John, but that is boring as shit.
JIM. *(Jim leans on the wall.)* Well, Jim is almost as boring. Wanna give me a new identity?
NEECHEE. No. I like the one you have. You're new in town, aren't you?
JIM. Yup. Flew in yesterday.
NEECHEE. So tomorrow's your first day at Joe McCarthy High?
JIM. Yup.
NEECHEE. Well, good luck cuz you're gonna need it. McCarthy High is a wild place and new kids are fair game. Don't matter to them how cool you are, they just wanna have somebody new to fuck up.
JIM. Hey, this is the burbs. These eyes have seen far worse than these green playgrounds ever will. *(Jim's arm L. to R. to Judy — turns hand.)* Who's that girl? *(Judy stands slowly.)*
NEECHEE. Judy Noonan. Better stay away from her — she's Buzz's chick.
JIM. So, Buzz is the big cheese around here?
NEECHEE. Yeah. And he could lacerate your face.
JIM. Bullshit. *(To Judy. Jim and Judy cross D.C., Kimberly stands.)* Your name is Judy, my name is Jim. I've got my eye on you. *(Jim crosses U. of Neechee. Judy crosses R. to L. of Kimberly.)*
JUDY. *(To Kimberly.)* Who was that?
KIMBERLY. Must be some new kid.
JUDY. *(In love.)* He ... he ... *touched* me. *(Judy holds Kimberly's hands.)*
JIM. Look at her. I'm a magician.

NEECHEE. *(Also in love with Jim.)* You can say that again.

COPS. Your parents are here. *(They fall to their knees.)*

KIDS. *(All cross to Judy, Kimberly, Neechee and Jim — three feet U. from edge of stage.)* I know, I know. I'm sorry. *(Pause.)* I'm fine. I'm fine. I said I was sorry.

JIM. *(Kimberly and Neechee join thumbs.)* I got drunk. I was mad. I don't wanna live here. *(Jim puts his head down.)*

JUDY. I can't tell you what happened. It's personal.

NEECHEE AND KIMBERLY. *(Neechee and Kimberly unlink thumbs.)* Not prison — probation. Prison the next time. *(To each other.)* Sure, *(To each other.)* sure. *(To front, sit back.)* There won't be a next time. I promise. *(Neechee and Kimberly raise their right hands up.)*

SCENE THREE

MUSIC VIDEO #2*

The kids get off their knees, say quick good-byes, exit, maybe slides of paradigmatic teens from the '50s through the '80s are shown as the kids set up their hangout — the construction site of a condo development called The Manor. Several stage images (all the standard fare of teen movies) show the passing of time and the growing relationships between the characters. Jim and Judy feeling growing erotic tension. Neechee and Kimberly wanting desperately to be liked by Jim and Judy, feeling easy acceptance by each other.

Jim and Judy cross Upstage Right into black. Neechee and Kimberly put on jackets, cross Center and look at each other. Jim and Judy exit Upstage Left and Upstage Right. Neechee and Kimberly exit Left and Right, poke out at each other.

---

*Suggested music: "Good Guys and Bad Guys" by David Lowry, Camper Van Beethoven, Jonathan Segal, Victor Krummernacher, Greg Lisher, Chris Molla and Chris Pederson. Performed by Camper Van Beethoven. See Special Note on Music on copyright page.

SCENE FOUR

THE START OF SOMETHING BIG

Neechee skulks around, looking out for the others. Kimberly approaches him from behind.

KIMBERLY.   *(Kimberly peeks out R. Softly.)* Boo.
NEECHEE.   *(Neechee peeks out L.)* She coming?
KIMBERLY.   She said. Is he?
NEECHEE.   He better. *(Neechee and Kimberly cross C.)*
KIMBERLY.   *(Neechee and Kimberly cross D.C.)* Makes me nervous, the idea that somebody that important likes me.
NEECHEE.   I know what you mean. Suddenly everything I do and say has extra significance. And I get hyper-paranoid that I'll almost taste Nirvana and then he'll get mad at me or something and it'll all vanish. I've been ignored for so long —
KIMBERLY.   — that being noticed better stick? I feel the same way. The two of us should make a confederacy, help each other stay wanted. You up for it?
NEECHEE.   Totally.
KIMBERLY.   Cool. *(They shake hands, tap bottom pinky. Neechee and Kimberly sit.)* You see him hold her hand in West Caf lunch line? Everybody got to talkin'.
NEECHEE.   Fuck. I envy him. Here less than a week and he's in the middle of everything.
KIMBERLY.   Big trouble is not the most rad thing to be in the middle of. Taking Judy away from Buzz ... he is headed for danger.
NEECHEE.   Danger bakes him.
KIMBERLY.   Well, he's cruisin' right into it. Mud raining everywhere.
NEECHEE.   His bike *(Neechee kneels and stands.)* is way more wicked than bike of Buzz. *(He kneels towards L.)* His bike is hard and lean and firm. It hums regal. It shines righteous. It is fierce and it is angry. They won't have to go half the trails before Buzz'll

kick out and dive the dust. History. *(To front. Stands.)* Jim *(He kneels towards R.)* Stark, the new king of Joe McCarthy High, will ride out glorious up the turnpike and into Pizza Hut, invincible.

KIMBERLY. He's just a guy, Neechee. He's a kid, even. He's not fuckin' Jesus.

NEECHEE. I wasn't sayin' that. *(Sits.)* I was just ... hoping.

KIMBERLY. *(Kneels facing D.)* Judy's the one holding the deck. *(To Neechee.)* She's the pivot. *(Slowly stands.)* It's her choice who wins, who loses — it's love power, not macho stuntwork that's running this game. In her hands, on her breasts, between her teeth — that's where victory is.

NEECHEE. *(Kneels with his head at Kimberly's chest.)* Who does she want? Do you know? She can't choose Buzz — he's a loser.

KIMBERLY. A loser on the inside track. A loser everybody thinks is a winner.

NEECHEE. *(Stands.)* That's what I'm scared of, Kimberly. That Judy'll pick Buzz over Jim because looks deceive. And fuck knows, it's an easier life on the inside track. They've bred us in this suburban wasteland to think that. I'm not sure Judy's ready to shed that skin.

KIMBERLY. So what do you want from me?

NEECHEE. What was first word?

KIMBERLY. She didn't give me first word. She told nothing.

NEECHEE. Whaddaya think, then? What's she gonna do?

KIMBERLY. Beats me. That's between Judy and the night. *(In the best of all possible worlds, Jim and Judy would ride up on a motorcycle or motocross bike just around now. An alternative would be to use a bicycle and motorcycle sounds. Or they could just walk on, to less dramatic effect. Jim and Judy enter L.)*

NEECHEE. Not anymore. *(Neechee and Kimberly cross D.R.)*

JIM. *(Jim and Neechee cross C.)* Good evening, comrades.

NEECHEE. Hey, dude. What's up?

JIM. Pummeled some guys. Got pummeled by some guys. *(Jim gives Neechee a "noogie.")* All in a day's work at Joe McCarthy High. *(Jim and Neechee exit L.)*

KIMBERLY. *(To Judy.)* Are you OK?

JUDY. Ask me after I down a brew.

JIM. Judy — where'd you stash 'em?

JUDY. In the tire. *(Neechee enters L. Jim retrieves the six-pack of beer.)*
JIM. Feel the groove! Six little gods. *(He throws beers to Neechee and Kimberly, then lustily approaches Judy, opens a can and pours beer down her throat. After a while, she pulls away, stunned but excited.)*
JUDY. That's enough, Jim. Don't want me to pass out, do you?
JIM. No. Don't want that. *(Jim and Judy kiss.)*
NEECHEE. *(He crosses L. of Jim.)* So what happened? How do we stand? *(Jim breaks the kiss.)*
JIM. *(Crosses D.C.)* What do you think? He's on top, I'm on the heap. Scatter my remains.
NEECHEE. *(Crosses D.C.R.)* But you've got his girl.
JUDY. That's not how I'd put it. *(Judy U. in model pose.)*
NEECHEE. *(Crosses R. to Kimberly.)* Fuck! Wrench in the works.
KIMBERLY. Seal it, Neechee.
JIM. I'm on the outside. Why is that so fucked? *(Jim crosses L.)* I've got a hang, I've got you guys, I've got brews, smoke, some Drum. *(Jim throws a Drum tobacco packet, a baggie full of pot and two packets of Bambu rolling papers onto the ground.)* What the fuck more do I need?
NEECHEE. *(Crosses to Jim.)* He's dangerous, man. He could shred you.
JIM. I could shred him.
NEECHEE. I know, I'm sorry, I meant ... he's got a crew of skaters and a crew of bikers. You've got us.
JUDY. *(Crosses to Kimberly.)* He won't listen. He's driving blindfolded and loving it. He's chasing the danger.
JIM. *(Lights a cigarette. Laughs.)* Listen to *her*. What a load of cheese.
JUDY. Jim, *(Crosses D.C.R.)* you gotta answer me. Now. What do you want? Do you want me, or do you want the danger of me?
JIM. Oh, go crawl back inside the TV, all you guys. My head is throbbin'. Listen. I'm cuttin' outa here, wanna think with my *own* brain. Kay? *(Crosses D.C.)* I need my self for myself. *(Judy crosses U.C. Jim crosses U.C. Neechee and Kimberly cross L. Jim starts off. Judy stops him.)*
JUDY. Call me? *(Jim stares at her, then exits U.L. with a beer can. Pause. Judy turns D. Neechee and Kimberly turn away.)* This is all total crap. I did not ask to be catch of the day. *(Crosses D.C., picks*

up a cigarette and searches for a light.) Two boys with oozing glands in a war over me, to get some weird power nobody understands. And do they care that I might not want either of them? No. The rules of the game are fixed against me. And I can't change the rules. *(She falls down at D.C.)*

KIMBERLY. *(Crosses to Judy with beer and lights Judy's cigarette.)* Who says? *(Kneels.)* Who says you can't tell them both to screw a tree? *Do* you want them? Because if you don't want them, then who needs them?

JUDY. Buzz is just boy. One boy no different from million boys. The only thing that makes him rise from the pack is his goddamn bike. Goddamn both their bikes. See, Jim is man. He's man of man. He's a loner. His heart and mind are his own. I do want him. But I wonder. Does he really want me? I mean, really want *me.* I don't know and I don't think I'll ever know. And it's eating me up inside.

KIMBERLY. Oh, don't let that happen, Judy. No boy is worth it.

JUDY. *(Puts away cigarettes in purse.)* No. I know. But Kimberly, I swear to you — this girl can't help it. *(Judy exits U.R. crying. Kimberly crosses U.C., crosses R., then gets a pen and paper from her front pocket and writes a poem.)*

KIMBERLY. Judy! Judy — come back! *(Pause.)* See you tomorrow. *(Neechee and Kimberly point to each other.)* Paper, rock, scissors — *(Neechee wins. He reads a poem that he got out of his backpack during the previous scene.)*

NEECHEE. *(Crosses C. with poem.)*

"To the One who Understands"
Slash and burn and fuck it all up
Slide in the dirt and talk to the earth
I will stand ten feet away
And watch your eyes cut holes through those traitors
I walk down those sterile hallways with a mask on
I put the cigarette and the bong in my mouth to keep from get-
        ting my face kicked in
Shutting out the shut down
Numbing numb numbness
Underneath the mask, I burn inside with anarchy and poetry
        and velocity and fire

And now suddenly, you've come to smash the enemy
You've come and I can take my mask off
And be free
(Neechee sits D.L. Kimberly crosses C. with poem.)
KIMBERLY.   "Bad Girls"
We're bad girls and we talk loud
We're bad girls and we stand proud
We're bad girls, hellbent for disaster
We're bad girls, runnin' faster and faster
We're bad girls, no boys will own us
Can't kill us even if you stone us
(Spit.)
Like Patti, I am an American artist
And I have no guilt
I will ride past the bad logic of suspender men and biker boys
and I will find the woman in myself
scrambled and trapped, gagging
underneath the bad girl
and I will take her out of the mire
and I will make her rich and red and real

NEECHEE.   That was really good.
KIMBERLY.   Yeah, well, I have a lot of feelings. I have to get
them out somehow.
NEECHEE.   *(Crosses to Kimberly.)* I know. Lots of times I get
these crazy rushes, like I'm gonna explode.
KIMBERLY.   Be careful, OK?
NEECHEE.   Careful of what?
KIMBERLY.   I don't know. People are weird. *(Picks up the beers,
crosses L., and steps back. Neechee exits U.R.)*

SCENE FIVE

TALK IN THE HALLS

Jim enters Right. Judy enters Left. They cross to Center. The halls of Joe McCarthy High. A bell rings. The kids carry books and cigarettes, combs and pot paraphernalia. Judy stops at her locker. Jim approaches. Judy and Jim cross Downstage Center.

JIM.   Are you on fire for me, baby? Are you on fire?

JUDY.   It's third period.

JIM.   You don't have fire in the morning? Not even in your mind?

JUDY.   You didn't call me.

JIM.   I don't use the phone. *(Crosses D.R.)* I use strength of will.

JUDY.   What do you think you are, some force of nature? You go to high school in the suburbs.

JIM.   *(Crosses to Judy.)* What do you think you are, some fuckin' queen *(Backs Judy into the wall L.)* of the universe? I could smash your face in.

JUDY.   You would, too. Bastard. *(Judy exits L. Neechee enters R. and crosses to Jim with backpack. Jim hits the wall L. and realizes that his macho overstatement has seriously backfired. He responds typically, spontaneously.)*

NEECHEE.   Jim! 'S it really gonna happen?

JIM.   'S what?

NEECHEE.   The tribal. I heard it's gonna happen tonight.

JIM.   Well, I think you're goin' deaf.

NEECHEE.   Oh, come on. You can tell me anything. *(Pause.)* Can't you?

JIM.   *(Turns to Neechee.)* It's not really a whole tribal, and we gotta keep it quiet cuz it's with knives and torches.

NEECHEE.   Scarring?

JIM.   Potential scarring. Scarring potential.

NEECHEE.   Holy. And you're not scared?

JIM.   Can't be scared. That's the whole point.

NEECHEE. Is she really that important?

JIM. Judy? Shit yes. She's crucial. Gotta have those lips. Gotta keep her lips away from his lips.

NEECHEE. To have power?

JIM. It's beyond that now. And it's beyond Judy. *(Turns D.)* It's something bigger than all of us.

NEECHEE. This is freaky, Jim. The tribal — they could splifficate you. *(Crosses to Jim.)* Make a wilderness and call it peace.

JIM. What?

NEECHEE. Please let me help you. I don't know what I could do, but I can't let you go it alone.

JIM. I like it alone. *(Crosses U.)* I appreciated your support, Neechee, you're my family, and I appreciate that. But alone is how I like to face things. *(Points to Neechee.)* See ya. *(Jim touches Neechee's arm, crosses L. and exits L. Neechee crosses D.C., and stares in vague amazement at his arm. Kimberly enters R. crosses to R. of Neechee.)*

NEECHEE. *(Softly.)* Family? Family. *(Kimberly plows into Neechee.)*

KIMBERLY. Second period, I got three different notes saying three different things. What in fuck's name is happening?

NEECHEE. *(To Kimberly.)* Tribal. Tonight. On the cliff. Knives. Torches. Him. Alone.

KIMBERLY. *(To D.)* A tribal? Alone? Nuh-uh, he's gotta be hiding a crew somewhere.

NEECHEE. No crews, I swear to you. He knows no one. He has romantic notions about loneness.

KIMBERLY. Lone stranger. Lone deranger.

NEECHEE. I can't tell what he thinks of her.

KIMBERLY. He'd better love her, or —

NEECHEE. Or what?

KIMBERLY. *(To Neechee.)* He'd better love her. *(To D.)*

NEECHEE. He says it's beyond that. It's beyond all that.

KIMBERLY. Like a war. *(To Neechee.)* Are you gonna go?

NEECHEE. To the tribal? No, he won't let me. *(Kimberly faces D.)* Maybe I'll watch by the fence, though.

KIMBERLY. We should all go up to The Manor and get stoned after.

NEECHEE. We should.

KIMBERLY. *(To each other.)* Are you keeping my secrets?
NEECHEE. 'Course. Are you keeping *my* secrets?
KIMBERLY. 'Course. And will you always?
NEECHEE. Always. And will *you* always?
KIMBERLY. Always. *(Both go D.)*
NEECHEE. I'll buy the beer, the pot, the chips.
KIMBERLY. I'll clear the coast, clue Judy.
NEECHEE AND KIMBERLY. Later. *(They shake hands. Kimberly crosses R. and Neechee exits L. Judy enters R. and Kimberly crosses to Judy. and Judy plows into Kimberly.)*
KIMBERLY. Judy — you're crying.
JUDY. Sixth period. Third floor Girls. Please?
KIMBERLY. Sure. Anything. Judy, what's wrong?
JUDY. Am I smearing?
KIMBERLY. Yeah.
JUDY. Shit.
KIMBERLY. Judy —
JUDY. Sixth period. Kay?
KIMBERLY. Yeah. No sweat. *(Judy kisses Kimberly on the cheek and dashes off.)*
JUDY. *(Crosses L. of Kimberly.)* Thanks a thou, Kimberly. You're the greatest. *(Judy exits U.L.)*
KIMBERLY. *(She touches her cheek, stunned. Softly to L.)* Greatest? *(To D.)* Greatest. *(She exits R. Jim enters U.L., turns back at C., exits R. Neechee enters U.L., exits R., Kimberly enters U.R., exits U.L. Together: Jim enters U.R., Judy enters L. with cigarette and Tab can. Judy sits L. Neechee enters U.R., exits U.R. Kimberly enters L.)*

SCENE SIX

GIRL TROUBLE

The Girls' Room. Judy enters Left with cigarette, sits on the floor, smoking. The bell rings. Pause. Kimberly enters Left.

JUDY.   Thank God. I thought you were never going to get here.
KIMBERLY.   Sixth period just started. I don't see what your problem is. Don't freak me out. *(She drops the backpack to her R.)* I'm here to help you.
JUDY.   I'm sorry, Kimberly.
KIMBERLY.   *(Kneels.)* I am, too. Seems like everybody's blowin' to bits, whole world's combustible.
JUDY.   My tears are making the world shake.
KIMBERLY.   They are.
JUDY.   That is so fucked.
KIMBERLY.   Just keep it minimal. Keep everything minimal.
JUDY.   I try. I — *(Sighs.)* I try to just live a normal life and it's all explosions.
KIMBERLY.   Strip it down. Get to the essentials.
JUDY.   But *you* think I shouldn't wanna screw either of them. Buzz *or* Jim.
KIMBERLY.   Well ... yeah.
JUDY.   And I think you're right. But I wanna screw someone. I've worked hard to get really nice skin and get the right style clothes. I deserve to screw someone. And here are two someones desiring me in a big way, I should probably screw one of them. *(Pause.)* I don't like talking like this. Tell me about the rebellious '70s. Tell me about Patti Smith.
KIMBERLY.   Patti Smith is a goddess in human form. Patti Smith said, "In heart I am an American artist and I have no guilt." Patti Smith was a woman punk rock star and she was sexy and had a hit single and did not shave her underarm hair. She read poetry between songs and once at CBGB's, the main place all the self-mutated punks bring their safety pins and attitude,

once at CBGB's, in the middle of a song, she fell off the stage and broke her neck and she went right on singing. Patti Smith's kid sister Kimberly *(She indicated herself.)* was supposed to become a rock star but didn't have the edge and never got her moment in the spotlight. In the song "Kimberly," *(She moves closer to Judy.)* Patti sings about being on a farm during a tornado a long time ago and holding her baby sister in her arms and how the sky was falling and she didn't mind. Because she could gaze deep into her sister's starry eyes. I love you. *(Judy hasn't been paying attention. She suddenly has resolve.)*

JUDY. I'm gonna do it. *(Judy stands.)* I'm gonna tell them to stop. I don't want a tribal in my honor. I don't want any of this bullshit. It's only sixth period. There's still time to do what's right. *(Judy stomps out her cigarette dramatically and gets ready to leave.)* Thanks for being with me, Kimberly. You're the best. *(Judy crosses U.L.)*

KIMBERLY. Goin' to The Manor later?

JUDY. Sure. *(Judy exits L. Kimberly stands.)*

KIMBERLY. Best. Greatest. *(She puts her backpack on her shoulder.)* The best doormat. The greatest asshole. *(She exits L.)*

SCENE SEVEN

LOVE SLAVES

Judy enters Upstage Left and crosses Downstage Right in black.

The road. Judy waits for Jim to roar by on his bike.

JUDY. 2:59. I just know he's comin' this way up the road. I know. He's comin' this way up the road and I'll feel it under my feet first, trembling; then I'll hear tree branches bending under the weight of air heaving past them, air in a shell shape, created by the power of the bike zoom. Then I'll hear the wall of sweet pain the bike shouts out down miles of roadway. And then I'll see his face. *(Jim enters U.L. and crosses D.L. Judy exits R.)*

JIM.   Machines roar between my legs. Tar melt or dust flood, the road takes me and my bike, takes us in and *fuck* it feels good. Riding the grind, kick jump to dive drop, breathing the road, the ride, the speed. Whole body hummin' from the seat of that bike, givin' it to the ground. Cuttin' it wide open. Almost there. What *will* she look like? *(Jim crosses to U.L. wall. Judy enters R. and crosses to U.R. wall. Jim and Judy acknowledge each other.)* Expecting me?

JUDY.   Yeah. Felt you coming.

JIM.   Felt you waiting.

JUDY.   Know what? I think you scare me.

JIM.   Why do you wait for me, then? You like me in spite of yourself?

JUDY.   Yes.

JIM.   *(He crosses to Judy.)* What in particular?

JUDY.   Same things I hate. *(Beat.)* Something's happening tonight, right? Some kind of catastrophe?

JIM.   Just a tribal. No big deal.

JUDY.   No big deal, just armageddon.

JIM.   Oh, come on, Judy. What the fuck else is there to do in this no name town?

JUDY.   Okay, then have your fuckin' bloodbath. And forget about me. *(Judy turns U. Jim puts his right arm on the wall.)*

JIM.   Listen, Judy. I know it's embarrassing, but I know you want it.

JUDY.   Yes yes yes. I want it. I wanna do it. But do I want you?

JIM.   Stupid not to.

JUDY.   Says you.

JIM.   How good does Buzz taste?

JUDY.   Why do you wanna know?

JIM.   How good does Buzz taste?

JUDY.   (Sighs.) ... Good.

JIM.   As good as this? *(He turns Judy's head to him and kisses her.)*

JUDY.   No. *(She kisses him.)* Stay. Come with me. Don't go off that cliff.

JIM.   Got to. Or I won't be a man.

JUDY. That's such bullshit.

JIM. Nobody'll think I'm a man. Nobody. And where'll that leave you?

JUDY. I used to think I loved Buzz.

JIM. And now you don't?

JUDY. Now I don't know what to think.

JIM. Neither do I. Till next we meet, babe. Kay? *(He kisses Judy and exits U.L.)*

JUDY. Shit. Till next we meet. *(She exits R.)*

SCENE EIGHT

PRE-TRIBAL RITUALS

The sun has set. Neechee enters Left and crosses Center with a lit candle in order to read a letter he has just written. He kneels.

NEECHEE. Dear Stranger,

I am alone inside myself. I am a lone loner lonely alone inside myself inside this school inside this town inside this State inside this society inside this world. I look out cuz in is too tiny — I look out and I see you. I see you alone, a lone loner lonely, looking out, looking for something real. Your eyes have extra penetration — you can make people like you. Strength and pride glow out of your eyes and saturate them, the ones that don't wanna know. They can't resist your power. And try as I may, I can't resist, myself. I fall limp and winded at your proverbial feet, ready to fuck anarchy and free will and just do your bidding. Your eyes — *(He can't really fathom having written this.)*

Your eyes blind me and I forget all logic, I wipe all the rules out of my brain. I can, in a tiny place inside myself, inside my lone

23

loner lonely self, I can love you. But then the world makes it petty demands. It makes me leave myself, leave your eyes and speak words, so then I follow the rules and do what you tell me and try to act like we're both just regular joes. *(Jim enters U.L.)* But sometimes I get lost in your eyes, so lost. Can't find my way out.

Yours always,

(Jim sneaks up on Neechee. Neechee holds the letter out, his arm outstretched, afraid to give it to Jim, not ready to give up and put it away.)
JIM.   You follow me here? *(He crosses D. to Neechee. Neechee stands.)* Some kinda sniper, or somethin'?
NEECHEE.   I knew you'd be by. *(Neechee picks up the candle. Jim lights a cigarette using the candle then Neechee puts the candle down.)* This is the only place they have tribals. Only place in town where there's water, fire and a cliff.
JIM.   What's up?
NEECHEE.   Special things you gotta do. Spit. Behind your left shoulder. *(Jim does.)*
JIM.   What else?
NEECHEE.   Put dirt behind your ear.
JIM.   Why?
NEECHEE.   Protects you. *(Both kneel. Jim puts dirt behind his ears.)*
JIM.   It's somethin' like thirty guys against me. They gonna kill me, you think?
NEECHEE.   Can't do that. Cuz then what else would they do?
JIM.   They gonna fuck up my bike?
NEECHEE.   Dunno.
JIM.   Don't know much, do you? You're on the outside.
NEECHEE.   Yeah. So? So are you.
JIM.   In a way, yes. In a way, no.
NEECHEE.   Already I've helped you out of a lot of jams.
JIM.   So?
NEECHEE.   *(Softly.)* Fuck you.
JIM.   *(He taps Neechee from behind.)* I love her tits, man. And I love that thirty fuckers barely know me wanna kill me. And I love

24

my bike and I love the weed here. And I love Led Zeppelin. I'm
ready for 'em, man. I'm goin'. *(He stands and crosses L; then shakes
Neechee's hand.)*
NEECHEE. Manor later? Victory party.
JIM. Sure. See ya later. What's that? *(Neechee pulls his letter-
holding hand away from Jim.)*
NEECHEE. Nothing. *(Jim exits U.L. Neechee looks at the letter and
tears it up; reaches for the candle. Music.*)*

SCENE NINE

POST-TRIBAL DEPRESSION

*Top of music, Kimberly unfurls blanket Upstage Center — 2nd
8 of music and takes off the backpack. At the 3rd 8, she dances
in a clockwise circle around the blanket, Panies; 4th 8 with
wild arms, etc.; and 5th 8, she is skipping with her arms.
Neechee enters Right with a bag of beers and puts it down Right
of the blanket.*

NEECHEE. Hey, Kimberly. *(Kimberly dumps the backpack contents
onto the blanket, and tosses the backpack L.)* Looks like you did a
spree. *(Neechee sits.)*
KIMBERLY. We're at the crux of what's going on — it makes
me hyper. I've gotta go take things, take what's mine. *(Stomps.)*
Listen — how long d'you stay at the tribal? Who's in the lead?
NEECHEE. I dunno. I left as it was starting. Don't be surprised
if they don't show tonight.
KIMBERLY. Why? What's the story?
NEECHEE. Think about it. All eyes are on them. All eyes. Why
should they give a shit about our eyes?

---

*Suggested music: "Add it Up" by Violent Femmes. See Special Note on Music
on copyright page.

KIMBERLY. We were there in their darkest hour. We nursed their wounds.

NEECHEE. But we don't have any power, Kimberly. Love means shit next to power.

KIMBERLY. Neechee, shut up. No Sylvia Plath pessimism on my time. We can be devious. Get Jim and Judy to fuck the system.

NEECHEE. No way.

KIMBERLY. Neechee, I think we're halfway there already. We snagged 'em. Everybody wants them and they want us. Judy was crying, her soul half shattered, and I'm the one who held her hand in Third Floor Girls'. I'm the one she wanted there next to her.

NEECHEE. So, you were first choice? You know that for sure? *(Beat.)* You don't.

KIMBERLY. No. But that doesn't mean —

NEECHEE. Kimberly, where are they? If they're with us, then why aren't they *with* us?

KIMBERLY. She's just late. He might be —

NEECHEE. Don't say it! Don't you dare say it! Fuck! Bad luck to think it, now I just thought it. You are fuckin' bad news tonight. And why'd you steal shit we can't use?

KIMBERLY. *(Stands.)* Fuck! *(She takes off her hat.)* I thought I left mom at home! Take your beers and get out of my face! This is Party Out of Bounds if I ever saw one.

NEECHEE. *(Stands.)* You call this a party? *(Neechee takes the beers and puts them D.R. Kimberly crosses R. Judy enters R. between Kimberly and Neechee.)*

JIM. Gimme a beer. Gimme a beer. *(Neechee gives Judy a beer. Judy can't get the cap off. Kimberly takes off the cap and gives the bottle to Judy.)*

KIMBERLY. Judy! Neechee thought you weren't coming. But I knew if you said yes you meant yes.

JUDY. He's not here yet. Fuck. Depths of danger.

KIMBERLY. No, don't worry. It's not necessarily —

JUDY. *(Not listening.)* I went by the cliff to try to see. Bastards wouldn't let me. *(Beat.)* Wouldn't let me *see*. Wouldn't let me *try* to see.

26

NEECHEE. What's goin' on?

KIMBERLY. It's OK, Judy. It's all right.

JUDY. So much screaming. Wild pain screaming. And they wouldn't let me see.

NEECHEE. Knives and torches. Thirty fuckers with knives and torches! I shoulda been there. Shoulda broke through.

KIMBERLY. Neechee, we have no idea what's goin' on. Everything could be fine.

NEECHEE. And everything could be over. *(Neechee takes a beer for Judy, crosses to the blanket and pours some on himself.)* Light a match, Kim, huh? Let me go.

JUDY. *(Confused.)* What's your problem? *(Jim enters U.L., slowly, dazed, disturbed, dirty, covered with feathers; maybe with his face painted in strange colors and crosses C. in [B].)*

KIMBERLY. Jim. Omigod. Look!

JUDY. Jim.

NEECHEE. JIM! Thank fuckin' Christ! *(Neechee runs up to Jim. Judy and Kimberly start to swarm him. Neechee crosses R. of Jim; Judy crosses L. of Jim; and Kimberly crosses R. of Neechee.)* What'd they *do* to you? Fuckin' feathers all over you.

JIM. *(Overlapping from "feathers.")* Outa my face, please, 'kay? Could ya back off? Huh? *(All back off.)* Where can I sit? *(Neechee and Kimberly clear a space.)*

KIMBERLY. Here.

JUDY. We thought you might be dead.

JIM. *(He sits C. Judy kneels L. of Jim.)* I can't talk now. I can't talk to anybody.

JUDY. You seem changed.

JIM. You have to go. They want you up at Friendly's.

JUDY. Who wants me?

JIM. The bunch of them. Lenore and Trixie said you have to.

JUDY. Marcy's birthday. Shit. I forgot all about it. I'm gonna catch hell. But I have to talk to you.

JIM. Go. Later we'll talk.

JUDY. *(To Kimberly. She crosses U.C.)* I have to go.

KIMBERLY. *(Hurt.)* Sure.

JUDY. Thanks for everything.

KIMBERLY. Sure.

JUDY. Sorry.

KIMBERLY. It's OK. *(Judy turns to Jim. She wants to kiss him good-bye, but it can't happen. She dashes off U.R., bewildered. Kimberly crosses R. of Jim and Neechee crosses L. of Jim staring at him.)*

JIM. I will tell nothing.

NEECHEE. Oh, that's OK. I understand. I'm just glad you're all right.

JIM. Can't tell. Can't ... speak.

NEECHEE. That's OK. Do ... Do what you want.

JIM. I wanna watch TV.

KIMBERLY. Have to go somewhere else.

JIM. Turn it on.

NEECHEE. Jim, maybe you need to get washed off first, get changed or something. You can't walk into your parents house looking like that.

JIM. Turn on the TV. Turn it on.

KIMBERLY. *(Overlapping.)* Wanna beer?

JIM. I wanna watch TV. I want you to turn it on. Turn ... I want —

NEECHEE. There's that pond over by the landfill. We could go there and you could wash off. And I bought some good hash today off Weasel. We could smoke that.

JIM. *(Stands.)* I'm gonna go back now. *(Jim exits U.L., dazed.)*

NEECHEE. Jesus, Jim. *(He backs against the L. wall.)* Take care, all right? *(Pause. Tentatively ...)* See ya tomorrow? *(Once Jim's gone ...)* Damnit. We've lost him.

28

SCENE TEN

RECLAMATION: STRATEGY

Neechee and Kimberly in different stage spaces (their bedrooms). They have portable phones. Music plays* while Neechee and Kimberly brood. Then the music fades out, then ...

1st "Dowah": Kimberly and Neechee have their hands up. 3rd 8, Neechee crosses Right and Kimberly crosses Left. 2nd "Dowah": Kimberly puts the blanket with the chatchkes in the backpack and crosses Right. Neechee picks up the bag of beer and crosses Left. Jim enters Upstage Left. Judy enters Upstage Right. Kimberly and Neechee cross Downstage Center, glare, and cross Left/Right at Downstage Center. Judy "party" Upstage Right; Jim "tribal" Upstage Left; both facing us. Kimberly crosses to Right. Neechee crosses to Left. Dance in ¼ time. Kimberly exits Right; Judy exits Right; Neechee exits Left; and Jim exits Left.

NEECHEE. *(Enters L. crosses D.R.)* I'm so mad, I'm so mad. I'm so mad I could shoot someone. But I can't cuz I'll go to prison. And I need to stay in society so I can change things. But what next, what next? Can't let it slip away, can't let my one shot at guy to guy friendship just go up in smoke. He's a real guy — one of the realest — and he makes me feel more like one myself. Can't let it slip. *(Kimberly enters R. and crosses D.L.)*

KIMBERLY. They've got her trapped. They've got her underneath their skins. She's sucked up into their Revlon world, their dollar earring world, their fucking Bennetton sweater world. She don't know; she don't know she's trapped — she's been breathin' poison air so long she thinks that's what life is. Outside is never easy but outside can be beautiful. She's seen that, she *knows* that. So why can't she *be* that?

---

*Suggested music: "How Soon is Now" by Steven Morrissey and John Marr. Performed by The Smiths. See Music on copyright page.

NEECHEE AND KIMBERLY.   Bus comes in two minutes. Strategy. Got it! Sex lure. Like in bug traps. [Kimberly!/ Neechee!] *(Neechee and Kimberly exit L./R., pick up phones and reenter dialing. They hear a busy signal.)* Fuck! *(They hang up. Neechee, more wired, waits a second then redials. Kimberly picks up immediately. Kimberly squats L. and Neechee squats R.)*

KIMBERLY.   Neechee! Gotta plan?

NEECHEE.   Party.

KIMBERLY.   Where? When?

NEECHEE.   My house. Friday night.

KIMBERLY.   Why?

NEECHEE.   Sanctuary.

KIMBERLY.   WHY?

NEECHEE.   They'll need it. To hide. To have sex.

KIMBERLY.   To be with us.

NEECHEE.   Away from Them.

KIMBERLY.   Parents?

NEECHEE.   No. Brazil.

KIMBERLY.   Utmost!

NEECHEE.   Sneaky?

KIMBERLY.   Not too.

NEECHEE.   Goin' for it.

KIMBERLY.   Beautiful!

NEECHEE AND KIMBERLY.   Later! *(They hang up. Neechee exits R. and Kimberly exits L. Judy enters U.L. and crosses C. A bell rings, Judy looks at her watch; then exits U.R.)*

SCENE ELEVEN

A HUSH IN THE HALLS

*Neechee enters Right and crosses Right facing Right with a
backpack. Kimberly enters Left, crosses to Neechee with a backpack and puts her hands over his eyes Right.*

KIMBERLY.   Guess who?
NEECHEE.   Um ... Vanna White?
KIMBERLY.   Close. *(Kimberly turns him around and hands him a
magazine photo.)* Here's the Iggy Pop photo I told you about.
Keep it.
NEECHEE.   Oh, thanks. *(Looks at it.)* Wow. Suitable for
framing. But I'll just keep it in my back pocket. KD was on TV
last night with all the anti-fur people. Told you she was a light-
weight.
KIMBERLY.   If you say so.
NEECHEE.   *(Pause.)* So we're not mad at each other.
KIMBERLY.   No. *(She hits Neechee.)* Guess not. Seen her?
NEECHEE.   No. Seen him?
KIMBERLY.   No. We better keep movin'. I'm gettin' desperate.
See ya Fifth.
NEECHEE.   See ya. Blue chairs in Smoking?
KIMBERLY.   Where else? *(Neechee exits R. Judy enters L. and
whisks past Kimberly calmly, hoping to be ignored. Kimberly crosses C.)*
JUDY! Christ. I almost missed you. You're going ... *(Softly, giving
up.)* so fast I can't keep up. Gone. *(Pause.)* Fuck! *(She crosses D.C.)*
I am *not* gonna let this lie. Come too close. So get ready for
adrenaline rush, Kimberly. Cuz here it comes. JUDY! *(Kimberly
runs off exiting R. Jim enters L. and crosses D.L. to his locker. Neechee
enters L. and crosses to Jim.)*
NEECHEE.   Finally found you.
JIM.   Finally? It's second period.
NEECHEE.   So now can you tell me what happened? I've gotta
know. *(Jim crosses D.C.R; Neechee crosses D.C. follows.)*

31

JIM.   Well. I don't gotta tell you.

NEECHEE.   Come on, Jim. I'm family.

JIM.   Shit. Some things you're better off not knowing. Crawl back under your shell, why don't you. Game over. *(Jim exits R.)*

NEECHEE.   *(Crosses D.R.)* Not so fast, buster. *(Crosses U.R.)* Not so fast. *(Neechee exits R. Judy and Kimberly enter U.R. and cross U.L., cross C.)*

KIMBERLY.   So did you pig out and have a Reesee Sundae, or did you have your usual Strawberry Fribble?

JUDY.   I have to get·to class. *(Judy exits L.)*

KIMBERLY.   Like hell you do. *(Kimberly exits L. Neechee enters R. Kimberly enters L. They both cross U.C., facing the audience.)*

NEECHEE AND KIMBERLY.   Next step: bathroom vigil. *(They both cross D.C.)* Check all floors, all periods, all day. Getting caught cutting six periods could mean detention, suspension or even expulsion. But it's a risk I gotta take. Won't make it through the day without another look. A chance to talk. To tell [him/her] how I feel inside. How much I feel. How very much I feel. *(The circle each other clockwise. Neechee exits U.R. and Kimberly exits U.L.)*

SCENE TWELVE

RECLAMATION, PART TWO: BATHROOM

Boys' Room. Jim enters Right, stands Up Center Right at urinal. Neechee enters Right and crosses Right of Jim; he fakes macho BS.

NEECHEE.   Jim! Fuckin' A. Gotcha.

JIM.   I'm peeing.

NEECHEE.   Well, I hope that's what you're doing.

JIM.   I'm pee shy. I can't piss now that you're here.

NEECHEE. Oh. Sorry. I'll go and then come back.

JIM. No, don't come back.

NEECHEE. *(Real again.)* What?

JIM. Don't come back. Best for all concerned.

NEECHEE. What ... Whaddaya mean? *(Jim has given up on peeing and crosses D.C.R.)*

JIM. The tribal changed things. Changed *me*.

NEECHEE. I know. I sensed it right away. Buy why —

JIM. They like how I fight. I'm on a higher echelon now. My relationship with Judy has been sanctioned. I'm in.

NEECHEE. *(Crosses R. of Jim.)* So?

JIM. So, think. Major stipulation of our agreement is that I steer the fuck clear of you. You and all outcasts. From now on.

NEECHEE. Can't believe it. It's me or them and you choose them? They're assholes. They tortured you.

JIM. There's more to it than that.

NEECHEE. What do you mean?

JIM. You wouldn't understand. *(Pause.)*

NEECHEE. Yeah, maybe I wouldn't. Cuz I guess I've misunderstood you from the beginning. I thought you were a rebel. I thought you wanted to raise hell. But I was wrong. You're not man of man. Never were. *(He starts to leave crossing U.R.)*

JIM. No, wait. *(Neechee stops. Pause.)* You're right. Screw them. I have the right to have my own friends.

NEECHEE. Only stand by me if you want to. I don't wanna be a charity case.

JIM. *(Crosses ½ U.C.R. overhand for high five.)* You're not. Not at all. *(Neechee crosses ½ D. Jim grabs Neechee's head, shoves C.R. and crosses D.R. Pause.)* What time is it?

NEECHEE. Ten to.

JIM. Fuck. Eight more minutes and I've gotta take a quiz in Snood's class.

NEECHEE. I have him seventh.

JIM. Do you think he's queer?

NEECHEE. Snood? I dunno. *(Pause.)* Why are you asking?

JIM. *(Laughs.)* Why do you think?

NEECHEE.   Oh. Then what makes you think ...

JIM.   Just lookin' at him. Fuckin' bow ties he wears. And what they write on the desks.

NEECHEE.   Never believe what they write on the desks.

JIM.   Yeah. Bet you're right. So, I'll see you around, I guess. *(He crosses U.R.)*

NEECHEE.   *(Crosses U.C.R.)* Actually, I'm havin' some people over Friday night. My parents are in Brazil for a month, so I figured I should start taking advantage.

JIM.   Shit. You shouldn't have people over, you should have *girls* over, *(He gives Neechee titty twister.)* you lucky turd.

NEECHEE.   I'm buyin' a lot of stuff from Weasel. And I can waste my Dad's booze no problem. So come by when you can.

JIM.   Sure. See ya.

NEECHEE.   See ya. *(Jim exits R. Neechee leaves the Boys' Room and heaves a huge sigh of relief and lust. He exits R. Lights up on the Girls' Room where Judy sits smoking as before. Kimberly approaches the implied Girls' Room door. She reads a poem from a crumpled piece of paper she holds. During her speech, Neechee crosses and stands at a distance, observing.)*

KIMBERLY.   *(She enters U.L. and crosses D.C.L.)* "A Letter to Judy." *(Judy strikes a match, lights a cigarette.)*

This letter is a poem because

I cannot make my feelings into grammar

I want the back-front-up-down-in-out-North-South-through-the-
    chimney-

down-the-drainpipe-any-damn-way-you-please journey of poetry

to take me through my longing for you

We share secrets and cigarettes

laughter and lingerie

tears hopes dreams desires

But I fear my desire for you far exceeds your expectations

We move in different orbits

A true collision could destroy the universe

But still I think maybe it could be beautiful

Explosions of the fireworks kind *(Neechee enters U.R.)*

Red boom blue boom white boom green boom purple boom

boom boom boom boom boom
And there'd be a new beginning
A new world
A new us

Yours most deeply.

NEECHEE. *(Crosses to U.R. of Kimberly.)* Just go in.
KIMBERLY. Neechee! You scared me. *(Kimberly nervously stashes her letter somewhere.)*
NEECHEE. She's in there. Just go in. Don't worry. You'll be super fine.
KIMBERLY. That's what you think. I think I'll be ploughed.
NEECHEE. *(He gently pushes Kimberly through the door as she resists, laughing.)* Just. Go. In. *(He pushes Kimberly into "bathroom" L. and exits L. Kimberly puts the poem into her backpack.)*
KIMBERLY. Hi.
JUDY. You're not here to piss, are you? You wanna talk to me.
KIMBERLY. Yeah, I do.
JUDY. Okay. But be quick. Lenore and Devry are due in here when Health gets out and they won't wanna see you.
KIMBERLY. Why are you scared of them? Why do you care?
JUDY. *(Crosses C.L.)* I'm not scared.
KIMBERLY. *(Crosses L.)* Are you gonna stay in here all day? It's not like you to mope around.
JUDY. How do you know? Do you know anything about me at all? No.
KIMBERLY. What's wrong?
JUDY. Why should I tell you?
KIMBERLY. *(She sits closer to Judy.)* Because I'll listen. *(Pause.)*
JUDY. *(Crosses U.C.L.)* Square peg in a round hole. I don't wanna be just one thing. Lenore, Marcy, Devry and them are nice and all, but they talk about one set of things. You talk about another set of things. I like that. That means I can pick and choose and become my own self. But they don't want that.
KIMBERLY. Do what *you* want. If you explain, maybe they'll understand.

JUDY. And maybe they won't. Kimberly, if I make a choice, my whole world could cave in.

KIMBERLY. Because the choice you want to make could make you an outcast.

JUDY. No, it's not just that. It's *not* that. Kimberly, I'm sorry I'm acting so queer. I'm just confused. And it's really for your safety. That gang — I've known them a long time. I'm tied to them.

KIMBERLY. Then break free.

JUDY. Don't wanna do that. Not completely free.

KIMBERLY. *(She decides to give Judy the note.)* I have something to give you. *(She roots around in a bag or pockets for her letter to Judy. The bell rings. Judy quickly gets up and gets ready to leave. Neechee waits by the implied Girls' Room door.)*

JUDY. *(Stands.)* Damn! They're coming and I don't feel like seeing them now. I'm gonna go to class. Come on, we gotta be quick or they'll see us.

KIMBERLY. Who cares?

JUDY. I care. *(Judy and Kimberly cross U., then cross U.C. Neechee enters L., crosses L. of Judy and Kimberly, catching them leaving the Girl's Room.)*

NEECHEE. *(Posing.)* Hey, babes. Just wanted to tell ya, serious party at my house Friday night with mega blitzing and sleepover possibilities. So I'd be crushed if you chicks didn't come.

JUDY. Is Jim coming?

NEECHEE. Yup.

JUDY. Cool. I'll see you then.

NEECHEE. Great. See ya, Judy.

JUDY. Bye, Neechee. Bye, Kim.

KIMBERLY. Bye, Judy. *(Judy exits R., reenters U.R., crosses D.L. Neechee and Kimberly face each other, laugh, do a high five. Neechee disappears. Kimberly exits R.)*

SCENE THIRTEEN

FACE OFF

Jim enters Left and crosses Downstage Right.

The halls. Judy enters Right and crosses Downstage Left, after bell rings. They see each other, then stop. At a distance ...

JIM. Hi.
JUDY. Hi. Are you all right?
JIM. Fine. I gotta kiss you.
JUDY. Not here.
JIM. Yes. Here. We're sanctioned now. Nobody's gonna give us any shit now.
JUDY. Sanctioned? What kind of bilious jargon is that?
JIM. Lenore didn't tell you? ... *(He crosses L.)* We all sorted it out at the tribal. I went through fire for them. So they decided to give me some rights.
JUDY. Rights to me.
JIM. That's not the best way to say it. An agreement. Contingent on you, course. On if you still want me. *(Pause. They kiss at D.C. Judy breaks the kiss.)*
JUDY. Tell me what they did to you.
JIM. *(He turns R.)* No.
JUDY. *(She is at Jim's back.)* Shit! Jim, you're sinkin' into a black hole and the harder I pull for you the deeper you slip. The whole school is making decisions that affect me. I think I deserve something in return.
JIM. Whaddaya want? *(He turns.)*
JUDY. I wanna understand your darkness.
JIM. *(Crosses D.R.)* Fuck. Talk about bilious jargon. I don't wanna understand anything. I just wanna blow out my senses. Fuck everything else. Ideas, feelings, the world. "My darkness." *(He crosses back to Judy D.C.)* Fuck that sewage. Get me high.
JUDY. *(She turns away and crosses L.)* I don't know you.

JIM. Yes, you do. And you love me. *(Pause.)* They want me to do the Minotaur Friday night. *(Judy turns slowly and crosses slowly to Jim.)* To test my virility or somethin' stupid like that. I'm thinkin' maybe fuck their noise. We could go to Neechee's instead and sweat in the dark.

JUDY. That sounds tasty. Beats the hell out of Friendly's. But all the more reason to keep a low profile till then. If Gang suspects we're cuttin' out on them, we're yesterday's news.

JIM. True. Harsh toke. So till then, Judy — simmer that flesh. *(He crosses to Judy.)*

JUDY. No words and no kisses till Friday night.

JIM. Wait! Not even one last? —

JUDY. No. *(She exits U.R. Jim crosses U.C., bends over and crosses to D.C.)*

SCENE FOURTEEN

MUSIC VIDEO #3*

As the song starts Neechee and Kimberly come Downstage and camp through the entire song for maybe just part of it, singing quite loudly. Sometimes they mess the words up and improvise words and conversation. Behind them, Judy and Jim (and maybe some techies) strike The Manor and set up Neechee's house. This is suggested vaguely, using a large red oriental rug, a big sofa and lots of junk food. Judy and Kimberly and Jim and Neechee each have moments where the intensity of their friendships are pushed towards the physical. Examples are boyish wrestling among the guys and back rubs and sisterly support through tears among the girls. Judy and Jim also have a stylized intimate moment and Neechee and Kimberly observe them as if they're an idealized dream image, then dance through and around them. Judy and Jim withdraw and this flows right into the next scene.

---

*Suggested music: "Kimberly" by Patti Smith, Ivan Kral and Allen Lanior. See Special Note on Music on copyright page.

SCENE FIFTEEN

RECLAMATION, PART THREE: SERIOUS PARTY

Neechee enters Left. Kimberly enters Right with candles, and puts them on the TV. Neechee throws junk food from Left to Kimberly.

KIMBERLY. So whadda we got?

NEECHEE. The most fabulous beverages and foodstuffs the American capitalist system has to offer. Cheetos, Ranch Style Ruffles, Pringles, some ludes, hash, Hostess SnoBalls, Jolt Cola, Entemann's Raspberry Danish Swirl, *(Kimberly takes the Jolt Cola and puts it U. of TV. Neechee gives Entemanns and beer to Kimberly. She puts the beer D. of TV, Entemanns on the TV.)* Molson Golden ...

KIMBERLY. Oh, cool.

NEECHEE. *(Enters L. with bong.)* and Dad's Johnny Walker Red, Beefeater, shit like that. Tom Collins mix. Oh, and Stouffer's French Bread Pizza and some Steakumms.

KIMBERLY. No Ramen noodles?

NEECHEE. Nope, sorry. *(He sits D. on the sofa and puts the bong D. of sofa.)* Maybe Judy'll bring some. If she comes.

KIMBERLY. *(Crosses to sofa, kneels U. of Neechee.)* Not this again. They'll come. Just not till late.

NEECHEE. They so know it's not a real party. Why should they come? What's making them?

KIMBERLY. They'll — ... Well, they'll need a place to hide out. No one will look for them here.

NEECHEE. You sound like the empath on *Star Trek* — how do you know what's gonna happen before it does?

KIMBERLY. Just a sense. It's not like all this stuff hasn't happened a million times before, at millions of high schools, on millions of TV shows. Why is it so weird to you?

NEECHEE. There's something you're not telling me.

KIMBERLY. *(Crosses C.)* Things are getting more intense with Buzz. He wants to test Jim's bravery and virility.

NEECHEE. *(Writhing on sofa with head in his hands, D.)* Kimberly, this is *so* not normal. This has *so* not happened a million times.
KIMBERLY. Don't blow a fuse over it. It's no big deal. Relax. They're coming.
NEECHEE. Let's write a poem.
KIMBERLY. *(Crosses to Neechee.)* Good — that's my Neechee. Got paper and pen?
NEECHEE. Wrapping paper and crayons. *(He exits L. and reenters with roll of paper and crayons putting D.C. on the rug. Kimberly sits D.L.)*
KIMBERLY. Excellent! *(She gathers food.)* Whaddaya wanna do? Exquisite Corpse or total collaboration?
NEECHEE. Let's try total collaboration.
KIMBERLY. Cool.
NEECHEE. Whaddaya wanna write about? The world or us?
KIMBERLY. Us.
NEECHEE. Okay. *(Kimberly writing. Neechee takes off his shoes.)* Clinging to little dreams and floating clouds of drug haze
KIMBERLY. *(Neechee writing.)* We drift in and out of fantasies and lies
NEECHEE. *(Kimberly still writing.)* Wishing ... No — Hoping for that shining moment of truth.
KIMBERLY. *(Neechee still writing.)* That white doorway that promises so much love
NEECHEE. — Wow. That's good. *(Kimberly writes.)*
We wait for an answer to our call *(Neechee sits up, looks at Kimberly, sits back down.)*
The cold response is no
KIMBERLY. *(Neeches writes.)* Shut out once more
NEECHEE AND KIMBERLY. Damned by a world we did not ask to live in. *(Shocked, they turn to look at each other.)* Spooky!*
*(*tingly fingers — this is the "spooky" gesture. They laugh. What follows is softer, more tender.)*
NEECHEE. I have the most fucking excellent time when I'm with you.
KIMBERLY. I have the most fucking excellent time when I'm with *you.*
NEECHEE. That's a good poem.

41

KIMBERLY. Damn good poem.

NEECHEE. *(He and Kimberly roll up the poem. Neechee puts the poem under the sofa.)* Don't really know what it's about, though.

KIMBERLY. You know. *(Pause.)*

NEECHEE. I always feel like myself when I'm with you. I think I'm in love with you. *(He leans into Kimberly.)*

KIMBERLY. No, you're not. You love me. You're *in love* with Jim.

NEECHEE. I can't believe you said that.

KIMBERLY. You're damn lucky I did say it. Cuz maybe in a few minutes you'll be able to. If I didn't, it might have been years before you came out of the haze.

NEECHEE. *(Leans against the sofa.)* How do you know? Do you think I'm faggy? Do you think —

KIMBERLY. I'm an empath.

NEECHEE. *(Accused, panicked.)* Oh, just shut up. Everybody's got excuses for shutting me out. I'm sick of it. The one time I felt like I was being myself —

KIMBERLY. *(Cuts him off.)* Neechee! *(Pause.)* Neechee, I love you. And I'm in love with Judy. *(Pause.)* I thought you knew. I thought you knew all of this. *(Pause.)*

NEECHEE. I did know. I didn't wanna know. I know he'll kick the shit out of me if I tell him.

KIMBERLY. Then he's not worth shit.

NEECHEE. But he is. I know he is.

KIMBERLY. Then maybe he *won't* kick the shit out of you. *(Pause. She crosses in to Neechee.)* We have to tell them. We have to *ride* this wave of power till it hits the coast.

NEECHEE. Meaning ...

KIMBERLY. We have to tell them *tonight.* And make sure they *listen.*

NEECHEE. Kimberly, no. Kimberly, don't make me — please!

KIMBERLY. Haven't you dreamed of it? Haven't you come *("Short word" charades gesture.)* this close?

NEECHEE. And gotten scared out of my skull. Kim, they slip through our fingers again 'and again from us just being outcasts. If they find out we're *queer* outcasts ...

KIMBERLY. We can't be scared. We can't list possible catastrophes. We must be valiant and forge forward into the dark unknown.

NEECHEE. You're right. Not telling is why it aches.

KIMBERLY. It could be beautiful. It could be so beautiful.

NEECHEE. Oooh. I can taste it.

KIMBERLY. Warm and smooth.

NEECHEE. Taut and slippery.

KIMBERLY. Best. Greatest.

NEECHEE. Closer than touching.

KIMBERLY. So, now, d'ya think you can go the distance?

NEECHEE. Yes. I have you inside my heart to help me.

KIMBERLY. Yes. And I have you inside my heart to help me.

NEECHEE AND KIMBERLY. So we're safe. *(They hug. Jim and Judy enter R. and cross U.C.R. with two bags of groceries.)*

JIM. Shouldn't leave the door open. Never know who's gonna bust in.

NEECHEE. *(He and Kimberly stand.)* Hey, you guys. Unexpected pleasure. Kimberly thought you'd be torrid late.

JUDY. We woulda been here sooner, but we forgot that Meat Farms closes at five. So we had to go to both Sev's. *(Judy gives the bags to Jim.)* Hey, Kimberly.

KIMBERLY. *(She and Judy hug U.C. Neechee crosses R. to Jim and they shake hands.)* Hey Judy. Didn't you guys have to see about business?

JUDY. What business?

NEECHEE AND KIMBERLY. Buzz business. (No *"spooky"* gesture.)

JIM. *(Triumphant.)* Blew it off. *(Beat.)*

KIMBERLY. Whatcha got?

JUDY. Same stuff as you guys, looks like. Plus Ramen noodles.

KIMBERLY. Torrid! Thanks, Judy.

JIM. Neechee, where should we put this stuff?

NEECHEE. On the floor's fine. *(Jim dumps the groceries on the floor at C. and puts down the bags U. of TV.)*

JIM. Thanks for havin' us, Neechee. We both need to chill out.

NEECHEE. Well, I'm hugely psyched that you could come.

JIM. Can we smoke some of that hash?

NEECHEE. Sure. *(He takes the hash from TV to D.C. and gives it to Jim. Kimberly crosses D.C. with the bong and gives it to Jim. Neechee and Kimberly sit L.)* Party hearty.

KIMBERLY. *(Under her breath.)* Gag me. *(Jim takes the pipe and the lighter, lights up, takes a hit and passes it to Judy. Judy takes a hit, then passes it to Kimberly and Neechee. Neechee opens the bag of Ruffles.)*

JIM. You know, I kinda like this scene better than the other one. They're just a mob — this is more like a family. *(Jim takes a hit.)*

JUDY. I know what you mean.

NEECHEE. That's how *(He passes the bong to Jim, leans on the sofa.)* I feel, too.

KIMBERLY. I feel stoned.

JIM. *(They all look at Kimberly.)* Off one hit?

KIMBERLY. Don't take much to get me thinkin' things I shouldn't.

SCENE SIXTEEN

MUSIC VIDEO #4*

Shotgun Jim to Judy, Judy turns head to Kimberly.

This is Neechee's and Kimberly's fantasy of their future with Judy and Jim. Judy and Jim are in an embrace that Neechee and Kimberly disentangle. Kimberly and Judy and Neechee and Jim dance and embrace and kiss in sexy and campy ways; an imaginary erotic ballet.

---

*Suggested music: "Take the Skinheads Bowling" by David Lowery, Chris Molla, Victor Krummenacher and Jonathan Segal. Performed by Camper Van Beethoven. See Special Note on Music on copyright page.

SCENE SEVENTEEN

REALITY

Back in reality. Neechee and Kimberly still longing.

JIM. *(All looking at Neechee.)* Neechee. *(Pause.)* Neechee? *(Beat.)* Neechee. Whatcha dreamin' about?

NEECHEE. Me? Nothin'.

JIM. *(Judy picks up the chips and crosses to the sofa D. Kimberly puts on shirt.)* Was that all your hash or is there more?

NEECHEE. There's more. *(Looks around, thrashes around.)* Somewhere.

JIM. That's OK.

NEECHEE. *(He stands and crosses D.R.)* Do you wanna maybe do something? Play truth or dare? Go out for a drive? *(Beat.)* Jim?

JIM. I dunno. Whatever. *(Stands.)* I'm gonna go piss. *(He exits L., seducing Judy before heading off.)*

JUDY. *(Stands.)* Kimberly, you still want that Ramen? Cuz I'm thinking of putting on some water now. If that's OK, Neechee.

NEECHEE. Sure.

KIMBERLY. Yeah, I'll have some Ramen. Sure.

JUDY. Good. *(Judy exits L. with chips. Jim and Judy take off their shoes and socks offstage. Kimberly stands and turns U.L.)*

SCENE EIGHTEEN

SECOND THOUGHTS

NEECHEE. They're gonna make out or something. Wanna sing show tunes?

KIMBERLY. *(Stands.)* No. I wanna talk to you.

NEECHEE. What about?

KIMBERLY. *(Conspiratorially.)* The way they're acting.

NEECHEE. What? Just like always.

KIMBERLY. That's true. But think about that. usually, do we ... *(She looks off U.L.)* — Do we let ourselves see what they're really like?

NEECHEE. Kimberly, you're talkin' in bubbles.

KIMBERLY. They're average, Neechee. They're not exciting. They reek of America.

NEECHEE. I know what you mean.

KIMBERLY. They like a certain kind of outside life, but they can't grok outcasts. Their social position is sanctioned, their love is sanctioned. They probably came here just to make out in ultra-plush haute bourgeois comfort with no 'rents or Gang to bug them. They're not really rebelling against anything.

NEECHEE. We're way nicer to them than they are to us — always. And they have their love, or whatever you'd call it, and they have that to lean on. And it gives them tons of excuses for not embracing us. They're like liberals. Deep inside, they wanna be like the mindless masses. They're not really dangerous.

KIMBERLY. *(Crosses D.C.L.)* Can we ignore these faults? Or are these faults proof that they may not be worthy of us? Have we just fallen for them because we have no better alternative?

NEECHEE. Those are big questions. *(Crosses D.C.R.)* But I think the real questions are: Can we live without them? *Will* we stop thinking about them even if we try? How long can we go without telling them before we burst?

SCENE NINETEEN

SOUNDS FROM OUTSIDE

Various loud noises are heard — first one at a time, then adding and overlapping in waves. Some of these noises are natural (banging, foot-stomping) and others are musical (drumming, etc.). The most important one is a loud drone from tuning forks or a cello E-string, meant to resemble the note struck at crucial moments in The Cherry Orchard. *When these noises repeat, the device will be simply noted in the text and all of the above will be applicable.*

NEECHEE. *(He and Kimberly turn U., and turn to each other.)* Merciless sewage! What's goin' on?

KIMBERLY. Attack. Attack at the back.

NEECHEE. All around. Everywhere. Surroundsound.

KIMBERLY. Too much. *(Jim enters L. terrified, turns and crosses D.R. with his belt undone. Judy enters L., also terrified, crosses D.L. pulling her pants up.)*

JIM. Holy fuckin' fuck! Found me. Found me out.

JUDY. Jim, what's up what's up what's *up?*

JIM. Comin' for us. To take us. To punish us. To change us.

JUDY. No!

JIM. Beatin' me down, beatin' me *down,* the sick fucks. Can't let them beat me down. *(The sounds subside.)*

NEECHEE. Now. Tell us. What is this? What's up? My house. No trouble. Tell me. *(Jim crosses D.C., D.C.R. They all cross to Jim.)*

JIM. Thought I could just run off and they wouldn't care. Guess I guessed wrong.

JUDY. Are they taking you now? They makin' you do the Minotaur now?

JIM. Think so.

KIMBERLY. Surroundsound stopped. What makes you think they're still there?

JIM. They're waitin' for me to act on my own.

NEECHEE.   How do they know we ain't gonna act on *you?*

JIM.   I don't get your drift.

NEECHEE.   What if I keep you here? *(Kimberly, Judy and Neechee try to stop him.)*

NEECHEE, KIMBERLY, AND JUDY.   *NO!*

JIM.   Just gotta tell 'em where I stand. If they think they can just steal me, they've got another thing comin'.

NEECHEE.   *(Crosses to Jim.)* I have a lot to discuss with you.

JIM.   Don't worry. Back in a flash. *(Jim and Judy cross L., kiss. Neechee and Kimberly turn backstage on kiss.)*

JUDY.   You be careful, now.

JIM.   I'll try to get you out of this.

JUDY.   Get us both out.

JIM.   I'll — ... I'll see what I can do. *(Jim exits L. Judy throws herself on the sofa. Neechee and Kimberly look at each other. Neechee sits D. of TV.)*

NEECHEE.   Something wicked this way comes.

JUDY.   *(She sits up on sofa.)* No it's not that bad really. *(Kimberly sits U. on the sofa arm.)*

KIMBERLY.   The two of you looked like a horror movie. Those sounds — totally bestial. And that's "not that bad?" Hate to see "bad."

JUDY.   It's just that — ... It's hard to explain.

NEECHEE.   It better be hard to explain. You're doin' a pretty shitty job of it.

JUDY.   Anything I say now could be a lie in half an hour. Wait. Just wait. *(Neechee crosses his fingers and arms, Judy lays her head on Kimberly's lap.)*.

SCENE TWENTY

TRUE CONFESSIONS

Jim is out on Neechee's lawn Upstage Center while the others stare out a "window" Downstage. Jim indicates that he's speaking to Buzz and a bunch of gang members.

Jim enters Left.

JIM.   Listen, guys, clear out. You're disturbing me. Me and my woman wanna be left alone ... No, we were *about* to scrog when you fucks had to come along ... Shit. I'm sorry, Buzz. Misunderstanding ... I'm sorry. I didn't know that was the deal ... No, that wasn't the first thing come into my mind. That you want to enslave us. I thought it was something more regular ... No, I don't want to forfeit her. I want her. I — ... I don't think she realizes that's part of the deal ... No, sir. *(Kneels.)* Sorry, sir. She loves you, sir. She told me, sir. She'll be glad to know you'll be punishing us. But, can I ask, sir ... what in case — I mean, *do* we have an alternative? *(Stands.)* ... Banishment? ... I see. Sir, if I ... Sir, may I go see Judy now? If I can just have some time, an hour, just an hour, to talk to her, to explain, then I'd feel — ... Yes. I know. I am ultimately alone. But can I — ? ... Thank you. Thank you most humbly. Thank you. *(He exits L., and reenters Neechee's house R. All cross to Jim.)*
NEECHEE.   Jim!
JIM.   Chill. Chill. *(Neechee sits D. of TV. Kimberly sits U. on the arm of the sofa.)*
JUDY.   Jim, what happened?
JIM.   Buzz just got this idea. We can't screw unless he gets to watch us and then punish us.
JUDY.   No way!
KIMBERLY.   Serious.
NEECHEE.   Grim.

JIM. We can only be together if he's watching. And half the school will be watching us to see if we break the rules.

JUDY. Jim, no *way!* There's gotta be an out.

JIM. Only out is banishment from everybody 'cept Kim and Neechee.

JUDY. No! So harsh! *(Beat.)* Oh. Sorry. I didn't —

NEECHEE AND KIMBERLY. 'S OK.

JIM. We got an hour to decide.

JUDY. That's tiny. Jim, what are we gonna do? *(She turns D.)* Caught between a rock and a rock.

JIM. *(He and Judy cross D.)* They won't even wanna pick fights with us. We'll be like lepers.

JUDY. Or invisible.

JIM. *(He turns D.)* Even worse. Invisible in Invisibleland. Nothing to do, nowhere to go.

NEECHEE. You can fuckin' stay here. This is a place. We love you.

KIMBERLY. We've been invisible our whole lives until that night in juvenile hall. It's a tough life, I admit. We make it through the day by the skin of our teeth, *(Stands.)* but goddamnit, we *make* it. We've found ways to color our world with beauty and speed and we drink our creativity and courage and it sustains us.

NEECHEE. *(Stands.)* Anarchy and outlaw status are two of the most beautiful things in the world. Please say you want them. Please say you'll stay.

JUDY. *(Crosses to Kimberly.)* We're more used to people liking us than you are. We're spoiled. It makes it harder.

JIM. *(Crosses to Neechee.)* I don't know. I don't know what I want, what to do, what to think. Everybody's pullin' me this way, that way ... You're tearin' me apart.

NEECHEE. That's the price you pay for reaching out to someone.

JIM. I always get in for free.

JUDY. Kim, Neechee — We don't wanna hurt you. We don't. *(Pause.)*

KIMBERLY. *(She and Neechee cross D.)* Neech, we gotta tell 'em.

NEECHEE. What, *now?*

KIMBERLY. Now or never.

NEECHEE. Secular saints preserve us!

KIMBERLY. We have the courage, Neechee.

JIM. What the fuck are you talkin' about? *(Neechee and Kimberly each gracefully take Jim and Judy aside, D. to talk. The scenes between same sex pairs are staged in the same way as the meeting scene.)*

NEECHEE. Jim —

KIMBERLY. Judy —

NEECHEE AND KIMBERLY. I have something to tell you.

JIM. Obviously.

JUDY. What's up?

NEECHEE AND KIMBERLY. I've been meaning to tell you for a long time.

KIMBERLY. I've written you letters and poems.

NEECHEE. I've gone over thousands of ways to say this again and again in my mind

KIMBERLY. Seeing you.

NEECHEE. Thinking of you.

NEECHEE AND KIMBERLY. In bed dreaming of you.

KIMBERLY. Almost saying the *(She and Neechee closer.)* words.

NEECHEE. Almost fixing your eyes.

NEECHEE AND KIMBERLY. Almost reaching you. I've spiralled out so far into the universe with my feelings for you that now there're no more words. *(Break. Neechee kisses Jim. Kimberly kisses Judy. This goes on for longer than anyone expects. Jim and Judy back off softly, R./L.)* I'm sorry.

JIM AND JUDY. No, it's OK. *(Pause.)* Kind of a heavy night.

NEECHEE AND KIMBERLY. Yeah, it's been a heavy night, and you're in love with [Judy/Jim] and everybody's watching you and you're scared about the future and I'm one toke over the line. Sorry.

JUDY. No problem.

JIM. It's no big deal.

NEECHEE AND KIMBERLY. But can I ask you ... to think about it?

JIM AND JUDY. Neechee —/Kimberly —

NEECHEE AND KIMBERLY. I'm offering you a serious alternative to slavery. Will you think about it? Will you? *(They all sit. Excruciatingly long silence. One at a time, they all light and start smoking cigarettes. Then the sounds begin.)*
JUDY. Shit. That's them.
KIMBERLY. No.
JUDY. FUCK! Jim, what are you gonna do?
JIM. Gotta go, baby.
JUDY. On his terms? You're really ready to go on his terms.
JIM. I don't mind his terms. *(Neechee crosses U. The sounds intensify.)* We gotta go.
NEECHEE. Not if they go first. I'm gonna get the gun. *(He exits L., and reenters with a gun. They all stand.)*
JUDY. NO!
KIMBERLY. Neechee! *(Sounds out.)*
NEECHEE. I'm gonna use the gun. *(Jim crosses D.R. Neechee stands on the sofa. Judy ducks D. of TV, and Kimberly crosses D.C. and squats.)*
JIM. Neechee, wait a minute — that's not such a good idea. There's lots of guys out there and they're dangerous.
NEECHEE. *(Near tears.)* Well, so am I. So am *I* fuckin' dangerous. I am so fucking dangerous you have no fucking idea.
JIM. Neechee, you're makin' everybody nervous flingin' that gun around.
NEECHEE. You risk your life every day for that shithead, why does a gun scare you? *(He sits on the back of the sofa and puts the gun in his mouth.)*
KIMBERLY. *(Near tears.)* NO FUCKING WAY, NEECHEE! *(Kimberly takes the gun C.)* How dare you. *(Jim takes the gun from Kimberly and puts it on the U. side of the TV.)*
NEECHEE. What am I gonna do, Kimberly? All my dreams were riding on him. Why *should* I go on? I'm so alone.
KIMBERLY. *(She crosses to Neechee.)* You're never alone, Neechee. I'll let it pass this time, but if you ever forget again, so help me. *(Pause.)*
NEECHEE. You won't do anything bad. Can't fool me.
KIMBERLY. No excuse. *(They hold hands. Tuning forks sound. She crosses to Jim.)* You'd better go. *(Jim exits L.)*

JIM.   Right. *(Beat.)* Shit. I have to gather talismans. *(Jim looks around the room for stuff. Kimberly approaches Judy.)*

KIMBERLY.   *(Crosses to Judy, kneels.)* You're getting married to a bunch of crazy boys. The odds are not in your favor.

JUDY.   I'll be all right.

KIMBERLY.   But it's not what you want.

JUDY.   Can I get what I want? No. Can I want? Maybe not.

KIMBERLY.   You're losin' your spirit, girl.

JUDY.   But I'll get sex.

KIMBERLY.   And I won't, I guess.

JUDY.   I wouldn't bet on it, honey. Not at Joe McCarthy High.

KIMBERLY.   That was acerbic.

JUDY.   Yeah. Learned *some*thing from you.

KIMBERLY.   Not enough.

JUDY.   I *might* get out of it, you know. With some luck.

KIMBERLY.   Oh? How? *(Jim enters L. with tortilla chips, lipstick and tonic water, approaches Judy from behind.)*

JIM.   Come on, babe. Let's go. *(Jim and Judy back off, U., ending up on the platform Right.)*

JUDY.   Bye, Kim.

KIMBERLY.   Bye, Jude.

JIM.   Bye, Neechee. *(Jim and Judy cross U. Neechee is silent. Once Jim and Judy are "outside," Neechee and Kimberly watch them from a "window" D.L. Music* plays as Jim and Judy perform various rituals. Each ritual is performed first by Jim and then by Judy, incorporating the junk that Jim has just picked up. First they strip to their underwear, then they draw lines and arrows on their arms and abdomens with lipstick, sprinkle tonic water on their heads, crush Doritos over their heads, light cigarettes and immediately stamp them out, breath long and softly on each other's necks. Then they turn their backs to the audience.)*

JIM AND JUDY.   Okay. We're ready. *(Disembodied hands and arms come from U.R. corner and grab Jim and Judy, whisking them off. Neechee and Kimberly turn away from the "window.")*

KIMBERLY.   *(Lying down on her back, rolls over.)* Well, off they go, into the sunrise. You OK?

NEECHEE.   Better. Sorry I scared you.

---

*Suggested music: "Wave of Mutilation" by Black Francis. Performed by The Pixies. See Special Note on Music on copyright page.

KIMBERLY.   'S OK.

NEECHEE.   Another chapter closed. Another revolution crushed by the State.

KIMBERLY.   And another will begin tomorrow.

NEECHEE.   Another chapter or another revolution?

KIMBERLY.   Both.

NEECHEE.   "Isn't it pretty to think so?"

KIMBERLY.   Keep your Hemingway to yourself. I think we'll be fine.

NEECHEE.   Who will we lust after?

KIMBERLY.   Nobody here worth the time of day. *(She kneels at C.)* How's about ideas? How's about we lust after ideas?

NEECHEE.   Which ones?

KIMBERLY.   So many different colors and sizes to choose from. Innate worth. The decline of civilization. Utilitarianism?

NEECHEE.   Nah. Sorry, Kim. Just doesn't work for me. Hate to say this, but I think we have to resort to porn.

KIMBERLY.   *(Spoken.)* Gulp.

NEECHEE.   *(Kneels on the sofa.)* And telling them was going to taste so delicious.

KIMBERLY.   But it didn't. And they were going to shun the band of the bland and the whole bourgeois American scene and stay with us forever.

NEECHEE.   But they didn't.

KIMBERLY.   You know what I think?

NEECHEE.   No. What do you think?

KIMBERLY.   Thinking about this whole thing, I think I must be very, very stupid. That's a secret.

NEECHEE.   *(Crosses to Kimberly, sits.)* Hmmm. You know what I think?

KIMBERLY.   No. What do you think?

NEECHEE.   Thinking about this whole thing, I think I must be very, very stupid. That's a secret.

KIMBERLY.   Hmmm. Now, are you still keeping my secrets?

NEECHEE.   'Course. Are you still keeping *my* secrets?

KIMBERLY.   'Course. And will you always?

NEECHEE.   Always. And will *you* always?

KIMBERLY. Always. (*Music.* They do a secret handshake: Kimberly fist, Neechee fist, on top, on top, pinkies, then dance. They cross U. into black.*)

SCENE TWENTY-ONE

CODA: FLASH FORWARD

The song continues to play as the actors enter one by one, pose for yearbook photos and exit. The following text can be recorded, spoken by the actor(s) who've done the cops voices, or spoken live by each stupid kid. Or you could use slides of actual year-book photos and text.

Jim enters from Right and crosses to Downstage Left.

Jim Stark graduated from Joe McCarthy High with a 2.7 average and is a junior mechanic at Better Auto Body. He lost his license after a drunk driving conviction. (*Judy enters L. and crosses D.R.*)

Judy Noonan graduated from Joe McCarthy High with a 3.2 average and an award for excellence in synchronized swimming. She is pregnant and unemployed. (*Neechee crosses D.C.R.*)

John "Neechee" Crawford graduated from Joe McCarthy High with a 3.5 average and the Dewey Whitehead Social Awareness Essay Award. He majors in philosophy and electronic music at Hampshire College and has two beautiful and talented boyfriends, a writer and a dancer. (*Kimberly crosses D.C.L.*)

---

*Suggested music: "Is It Really So Strange" by John Marr and Steven Morrissey. Performed by The Smiths. See Special Note on Music on copyright page.

Jane "Kimberly Willis" graduated Joe McCarthy High with a 3.7 average and the Linda Velzy Memorial Award for Creative Writing. She lives in San Francisco with her cats Patsy and Colette, and bakes bread for a vegetarian restaurant. She is a member of the activist groups Queer Nation and ACT UP and this afternoon, while walking home from karate class with a friend, she fell in love.

THE END

(Curtain call: All bow two times. They dance to U.C. in black: Kimberly exits L., Neechee exits R., Jim exits U.L. and Judy exits U.R. All enter on key note. They bow, "spooky" gesture. Jim and Judy exit U.L./U.R., Kimberly and Neechee cross U.C.L./U.C.R., "spooky" to each other, then exit U.L./U.R.)

STUPID KIDS
APPENDIX A

"Stupid Kids" by Dan Selzman, Elizabeth Cox, Michael Cudahy and Peter Rutigliano.
Performed by Christmas.
Bugle Publishing
14724 Ventura Boulevard, PH
Sherman Oaks, CA 91403
Attn: Ms Karen Ahmed
Telephone: (818) 461-1707
Facsimile: (818) 461-1739

"Good Guys and Bad Guys" by David Lowry, Camper Van Beethoven, Jonathan Segal, Victor Krummernacher, Greg Lisher, Chris Molla and Chris Pederson.
Performed by
Camper Van Beethoven.
Bug Music
6777 Hollywood Boulevard
Hollywood, CA 90028
Attn: Ms Pamela Lillig James
Telephone: (213) 466-4352
Facsimile: (213) 466-2366

"Add it Up" by Violent Femmes
Gorno Music
c/o Alan N. Skiena, Esq.
1370 Avenue of the Americas, Suite 2701
New York, NY 10019
Telephone: (212) 664-1131
Facsimile: (212) 582-9713

"How Soon is Now" by Steven Morrissey and John Marr.
Performed by The Smiths. "Is It Really So Strange" by John Marr

and Steven Morrissey.
Performed by The Smiths.
Warner-Chappell Music, Warner-Tamerlane Music Publishing
10585 Santa Monica Boulevard
Los Angeles, CA 90025-4950
Attn: April Franks
Telephone: (310) 441-6800
Facsimile: (310) 470-6399

"Kimberly" by Patti Smith, Ivan Kral, and Allen Lanier
RZO Publishing
110 West 57th Street
New York, NY 10019
Attn: Mr. Henry Wrenn-Meleck
Telephone: (212) 765-7557
Facsimile: (212) 245-2356

"Take the Skinheads Bowling" by David Lowry, Chris Molla, Victor Krummenacher and Jonathan Segal. Performed by Camper van Beethoven.
Independent Project Music
23564 Calibasis Road, Suite 107
Calibasis, CA 91302
Attn: Mr. Randall Wixen
Telephone: (818) 591-7335
Facsimile: (818) 591-7178

"Wave of Mutilation" by Black Francis. Performed by The Pixies.
Rice & Beans Music
179 Jordan Road
Dartmouth, MA 02748
Attn: Mr. Ken Goes
Telephone: (508) 636-3334
Facsimile: (508) 636-3332

NEW PLAYS

★ HONOUR by Joanna Murray-Smith. In a series of intense confrontations, a wife, husband, lover and daughter negotiate the forces of passion, history, responsibility and honour. "HONOUR makes for surprisingly interesting viewing. Tight, crackling dialogue (usually played out in punchy verbal duels) captures characters unable to deal with emotions ... Murray-Smith effectively places her characters in situations that strip away pretense." –Variety "... the play's virtues are strong: a distinctive theatrical voice, passionate concerns ... HONOUR might just capture a few honors of its own." –Time Out Magazine [1M, 3W] ISBN: 0-8222-1683-3

★ MR. PETERS' CONNECTIONS by Arthur Miller. Mr. Miller describes the protagonist as existing in a dream-like state when the mind is "freed to roam from real memories to conjectures, from trivialities to tragic insights, from terror of death to glorying in one's being alive." With this memory play, the Tony Award and Pulitzer Prize-winner reaffirms his stature as the world's foremost dramatist. "... a cross between Joycean stream-of-consciousness and Strindberg's dream plays, sweetened with a dose of William Saroyan's philosophical whimsy ... CONNECTIONS is most intriguing ..." –The NY Times [5M, 3W] ISBN: 0-8222-1687-6

★ THE WAITING ROOM by Lisa Loomer. Three women from different centuries meet in a doctor's waiting room in this dark comedy about the timeless quest for beauty – and its cost. "... THE WAITING ROOM ... is a bold, risky melange of conflicting elements that is ... terrifically moving ... There's no resisting the fierce emotional pull of the play." –The NY Times "... one of the high points of this year's Off-Broadway season ... THE WAITING ROOM is well worth a visit." –Back Stage [7M, 4W, flexible casting] ISBN: 0-8222-1594-2

★ THE OLD SETTLER by John Henry Redwood. A sweet-natured comedy about two church-going sisters in 1943 Harlem and the handsome young man who rents a room in their apartment. "For all of its decent sentiments, THE OLD SETTLER avoids sentimentality. It has the authenticity and lack of pretense of an Early American sampler." –The NY Times "We've had some fine plays Off-Broadway this season, and this is one of the best." –The NY Post [1M, 3W] ISBN: 0-8-222-1642-6

★ LAST TRAIN TO NIBROC by Arlene Hutton. In 1940 two young strangers share a seat on a train bound east only to find their paths will cross again. "All aboard. LAST TRAIN TO NIBROC is a sweetly told little chamber romance." –Show Business "... [a] gently charming little play, reminiscent of Thornton Wilder in its look at rustic Americans who are to be treasured for their simplicity and directness ..." –Associated Press "The old formula of boy wins girls, boy loses girl, boy wins girl still works ... [a] well-made play that perfectly captures a slice of small-town-life-gone-by." –Back Stage [1M, 1W] ISBN: 0-8222-1753-8

★ OVER THE RIVER AND THROUGH THE WOODS by Joe DiPietro. Nick sees both sets of his grandparents every Sunday for dinner. This is routine until he has to tell them that he's been offered a dream job in Seattle. The news doesn't sit so well. "A hilarious family comedy that is even funnier than his long running musical revue I Love You, You're Perfect, Now Change." –Back Stage "Loaded with laughs every step of the way." –Star-Ledger [3M, 3W] ISBN: 0-8222-1712-0

★ SIDE MAN by Warren Leight. 1999 Tony Award winner. This is the story of a broken family and the decline of jazz as popular entertainment. "... a tender, deeply personal memory play about the turmoil in the family of a jazz musician as his career crumbles at the dawn of the age of rock-and-roll ..." –The NY Times "[SIDE MAN] is an elegy for two things – a lost world and a lost love. When the two notes sound together in harmony, it is moving and graceful ..." –The NY Daily News "An atmospheric memory play ... with crisp dialogue and clearly drawn characters ... reflects the passing of an era with persuasive insight ... The joy and despair of the musicians is skillfully illustrated." –Variety [5M, 3W] ISBN: 0-8222-1721-X

DRAMATISTS PLAY SERVICE, INC.
440 Park Avenue South, New York, NY 10016 212-683-8960 Fax 212-213-1539
postmaster@dramatists.com   www.dramatists.com

NEW PLAYS

★ **CLOSER by Patrick Marber.** Winner of the 1998 Olivier Award for Best Play and the 1999 New York Drama Critics Circle Award for Best Foreign Play. Four lives intertwine over the course of four and a half years in this densely plotted, stinging look at modern love and betrayal. "CLOSER is a sad, savvy, often funny play that casts a steely, unblinking gaze at the world of relationships and lets you come to your own conclusions ... CLOSER does not merely hold your attention; it burrows into you." –*New York Magazine* "A powerful, darkly funny play about the cosmic collision between the sun of love and the comet of desire." –*Newsweek Magazine* [2M, 2W] ISBN: 0-8222-1722-8

★ **THE MOST FABULOUS STORY EVER TOLD by Paul Rudnick.** A stage manager, headset and prompt book at hand, brings the house lights to half, then dark, and cues the creation of the world. Throughout the play, she's in control of everything. In other words, she's either God, or she thinks she is. "Line by line, Mr. Rudnick may be the funniest writer for the stage in the United States today ... One-liners, epigrams, withering put-downs and flashing repartee: These are the candles that Mr. Rudnick lights instead of cursing the darkness ... a testament to the virtues of laughing ... and in laughter, there is something like the memory of Eden." –*The NY Times* "Funny it is ... consistently, rapaciously, deliriously ... easily the funniest play in town." –*Variety* [4M, 5W] ISBN: 0-8222-1720-1

★ **A DOLL'S HOUSE by Henrik Ibsen, adapted by Frank McGuinness.** Winner of the 1997 Tony Award for Best Revival. "New, raw, gut-twisting and gripping. Easily the hottest drama this season." –*USA Today* "Bold, brilliant and alive." –*The Wall Street Journal* "A thunderclap of an evening that takes your breath away." –*Time Magazine* [4M, 4W, 2 boys] ISBN: 0-8222-1636-1

★ **THE HERBAL BED by Peter Whelan.** The play is based on actual events which occurred in Stratford-upon-Avon in the summer of 1613, when William Shakespeare's elder daughter was publicly accused of having a sexual liaison with a married neighbor and family friend. "In his probing new play, THE HERBAL BED ... Peter Whelan muses about a sidelong event in the life of Shakespeare's family and creates a finely textured tapestry of love and lies in the early 17th-century Stratford." –*The NY Times* "It is a first rate drama with interesting moral issues of truth and expediency." –*The NY Post* [5M, 3W] ISBN: 0-8222-1675-2

★ **SNAKEBIT by David Marshall Grant.** A study of modern friendship when put to the test. "... a rather smart and absorbing evening of water-cooler theater, the intimate sort of Off-Broadway experience that has you picking apart the recognizable characters long after the curtain calls." –*The NY Times* "Off-Broadway keeps on presenting us with compelling reasons for going to the theater. The latest is SNAKEBIT, David Marshall Grant's smart new comic drama about being thirtysomething and losing one's way in life." –*The NY Daily News* [3M, 1W] ISBN: 0-8222-1724-4

★ **A QUESTION OF MERCY by David Rabe.** The Obie Award-winning playwright probes the sensitive and controversial issue of doctor-assisted suicide in the age of AIDS in this poignant drama. "There are many devastating ironies in Mr. Rabe's beautifully considered, piercingly clear-eyed work ..." –*The NY Times* "With unsettling candor and disturbing insight, the play arouses pity and understanding of a troubling subject ... Rabe's provocative tale is an affirmation of dignity that rings clear and true." –*Variety* [6M, 1W] ISBN: 0-8222-1643-4

★ **DIMLY PERCEIVED THREATS TO THE SYSTEM by Jon Klein.** Reality and fantasy overlap with hilarious results as this unforgettable family attempts to survive the nineties. "Here's a play whose point about fractured families goes to the heart, mind – and ears." –*The Washington Post* "... an end-of-the-millennium comedy about a family on the verge of a nervous breakdown ... Trenchant and hilarious ..." –*The Baltimore Sun* [2M, 4W] ISBN: 0-8222-1677-9

DRAMATISTS PLAY SERVICE, INC.
440 Park Avenue South, New York, NY 10016 212-683-8960 Fax 212-213-1539
postmaster@dramatists.com www.dramatists.com

NEW PLAYS

★ **AS BEES IN HONEY DROWN by Douglas Carter Beane.** Winner of the John Gassner Playwriting Award. A hot young novelist finds the subject of his new screenplay in a New York socialite who leads him into the world of *Auntie Mame* and *Breakfast at Tiffany's*, before she takes him for a ride. "A delicious soufflé of a satire ... [an] extremely entertaining fable for an age that always chooses image over substance." *—The NY Times* "... A witty assessment of one of the most active and relentless industries in a consumer society ... the creation of 'hot' young things, which the media have learned to mass produce with efficiency and zeal." *—The NY Daily News* [3M, 3W, flexible casting] ISBN: 0-8222-1651-5

★ **STUPID KIDS by John C. Russell.** In rapid, highly stylized scenes, the story follows four high-school students as they make their way from first through eighth period and beyond, struggling with the fears, frustrations, and longings peculiar to youth. "In STUPID KIDS ... playwright John C. Russell gets the opera of adolescence to a T ... The stylized teenspeak of STUPID KIDS ... suggests that Mr. Russell may have hidden a tape recorder under a desk in study hall somewhere and then scoured the tapes for good quotations ... it is the kids' insular, ceaselessly churning world, a pre-adult world of Doritos and libidos, that the playwright seeks to lay bare." *—The NY Times* "STUPID KIDS [is] a sharp-edged ... whoosh of teen angst and conformity anguish. It is also very funny." *—NY Newsday* [2M, 2W] ISBN: 0-8222-1698-1

★ **COLLECTED STORIES by Donald Margulies.** From Obie Award-winner Donald Margulies comes a provocative analysis of a student-teacher relationship that turns sour when the protégé becomes a rival. "With his fine ear for detail, Margulies creates an authentic, insular world, and he gives equal weight to the opposing viewpoints of two formidable characters." *—The LA Times* "This is probably Margulies' best play to date ..." *—The NY Post* "... always fluid and lively, the play is thick with ideas, like a stock-pot of good stew." *—The Village Voice* [2W] ISBN: 0-8222-1640-X

★ **FREEDOMLAND by Amy Freed.** An overdue showdown between a son and his father sets off fireworks that illuminate the neurosis, rage and anxiety of one family – and of America at the turn of the millennium. "FREEDOMLAND's more obvious links are to *Buried Child* and *Bosoms and Neglect*. Freed, like Guare, is an inspired wordsmith with a gift for surreal touches in situations grounded in familiar and real territory." *—Curtain Up* [3M, 4W] ISBN: 0-8222-1719-8

★ **STOP KISS by Diana Son.** A poignant and funny play about the ways, both sudden and slow, that lives can change irrevocably. "There's so much that is vital and exciting about STOP KISS ... you want to embrace this young author and cheer her onto other works ... the writing on display here is funny and credible ... you also will be charmed by its heartfelt characters and up-to-the-minute humor." *—The NY Daily News* "... irresistibly exciting ... a sweet, sad, and enchantingly sincere play." *—The NY Times* [3M, 3W] ISBN: 0-8222-1731-7

★ **THREE DAYS OF RAIN by Richard Greenberg.** The sins of fathers and mothers make for a bittersweet elegy in this poignant and revealing drama. "... a work so perfectly judged it heralds the arrival of a major playwright ... Greenberg is extraordinary." *—The NY Daily News* "Greenberg's play is filled with graceful passages that are by turns melancholy, harrowing, and often, quite funny." *—Variety* [2M, 1W] ISBN: 0-8222-1676-0

★ **THE WEIR by Conor McPherson.** In a bar in rural Ireland, the local men swap spooky stories in an attempt to impress a young woman from Dublin who recently moved into a nearby "haunted" house. However, the tables are soon turned when she spins a yarn of her own. "You shed all sense of time at this beautiful and devious new play." *—The NY Times* "Sheer theatrical magic. I have rarely been so convinced that I have just seen a modern classic. Tremendous." *—The London Daily Telegraph* [4M, 1W] ISBN: 0-8222-1706-6

DRAMATISTS PLAY SERVICE, INC.
440 Park Avenue South, New York, NY 10016 212-683-8960 Fax 212-213-1539
postmaster@dramatists.com www.dramatists.com